AMY KLOBUCHAR
UNITED STATES SENATOR
FROM MINNESOTA

The

2020

★★★ **DEMOCRATIC** ★★★

PRESIDENTIAL CANDIDATES

COLORING *and* ACTIVITY BOOK

SONYA SATURDAY

TILLER PRESS

NEW YORK LONDON TORONTO SYDNEY NEW DELHI

TILLER PRESS

An Imprint of Simon & Schuster, Inc.
1230 Avenue of the Americas
New York, NY 10020

First Tiller Press trade paperback edition January 2020

TILLER PRESS and colophon are trademarks of Simon & Schuster, Inc.

For information about special discounts for bulk purchases, please contact
Simon & Schuster Special Sales at 1-866-506-1949 or business@simonandschuster.com

The Simon & Schuster Speakers Bureau can bring authors to your live event.
For more information or to book an event contact the Simon & Schuster Speakers Bureau
at 1-866-248-3049 or visit our website at www.simonspeakers.com.

Interior design and jacket art by Sonya Saturday

Manufactured in the United States of America

10 9 8 7 6 5 4 3 2 1

ISBN 978-1-9821-4225-4

BERNIE SANDERS
UNITED STATES SENATOR
FROM VERMONT

JOHN DELANEY
*FORMER UNITED STATES
REPRESENTATIVE FROM
MARYLAND*

ANDREW YANG

ENTREPRENEUR

JOE SESTAK
FORMER UNITED STATES
REPRESENTATIVE
FROM PENNSYLVANIA

BETO O'ROURKE
FORMER UNITED STATES
REPRESENTATIVE FROM TEXAS

ELIZABETH WARREN
UNITED STATES SENATOR
FROM MASSACHUSETTS

MICHAEL BENNET
UNITED STATES SENATOR
FROM COLORADO

BILL DE BLASIO
MAYOR OF NEW YORK CITY

JOHN HICKENLOOPER

*FORMER GOVERNOR
OF COLORADO*

PRESIDENTIAL BEHAVIOR

Match the following nicknames given by Donald Trump to the appropriate Democratic candidate.

1) SleepyCreepy	A) Kirsten Gillibrand
2) Alfred E. Neuman	B) Bernie Sanders
3) Lightweight Senator	C) Pete Buttigieg
4) The Nutty Professor	D) Elizabeth Warren
5) Pocahontas	E) Joe Biden

Answer: 1) E, 2) C, 3) A, 4) B, 5) D

KAMALA HARRIS
UNITED STATES SENATOR
FROM CALIFORNIA

PETE BUTTIGIEG
MAYOR OF SOUTH BEND, INDIANA

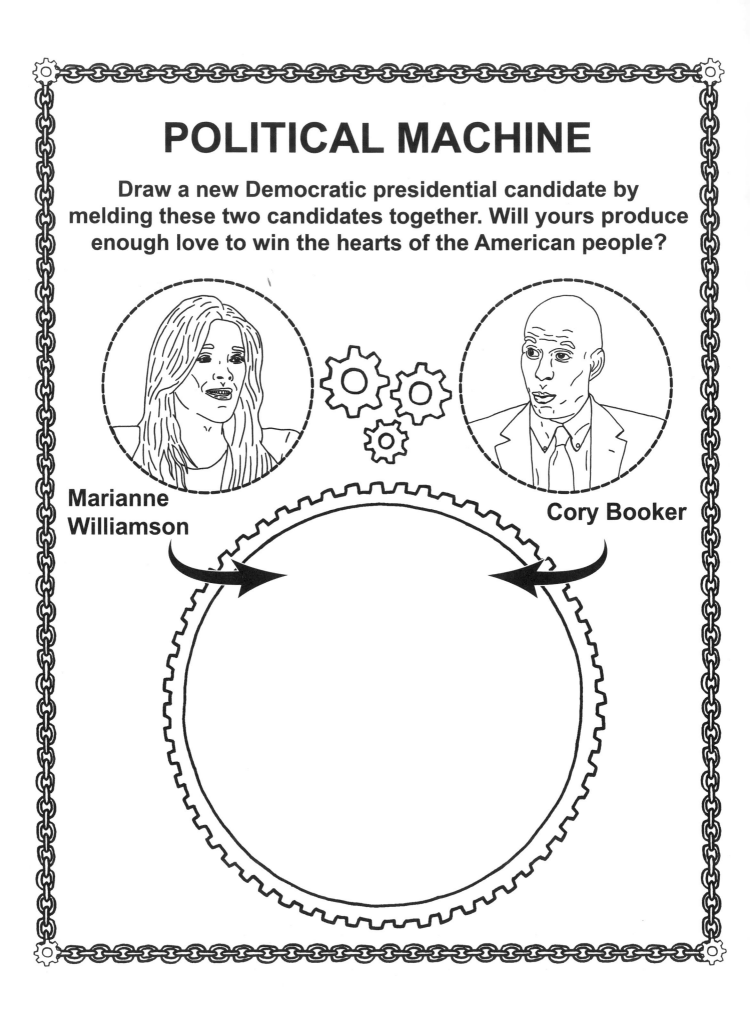

ERIC SWALWELL
UNITED STATES REPRESENTATIVE
FROM CALIFORNIA

CAMPAIGN ISSUES

Search the puzzle for these phrases that matter to the Democratic Party. Issues can be up, down, forward, backward, and diagonal, so good luck connecting with voters!

INCOME INEQUALITY

CRIMINAL JUSTICE REFORM

MEDICARE FOR ALL

STUDENT DEBT

CAMPAIGN FINANCE

ELECTORAL COLLEGE

REDUCING CARBON EMISSIONS

CLIMATE CHANGE

BACKGROUND CHECKS

TRANSPORTATION

WEALTH TAXES

ONLINE PRIVACY

A T G C R I M I N A L J U S T I C E R E F O R M
Q Y A K O D A B S I P M U R T T O N E S A E L P
A O J R Z Q M O S J Y P N M Y P X O O M D E F L
U N G N I H T Y R E V E S N I U R P M U R T U A
G I Q M P X U X T N F M A Y K L L P C Q W G R H
X A A S K N I T S P M U R T E L B I R R E T B I
H G P L I G P M U R T E K I L T N O D I A S W F
C A M P A I G N F I N A N C E G H T Q Q L K U O
S P U M M Y R V G L D V G B C N N W Q B T E Q T
A M R T T R A N S P O R T A T I O N L U H U G B
V U T D U P W F B S H B R C O P B O J T T U X A
G R L O Z B R D D I W B P K R P M M M X R A G Q Q
A T L N Q R F L T I O A G G A O K O M U X X M B
R H I L P J G I B N N Q K R L E M R S M E U P O
M Y T I L A U Q E N I E M O C N I E P P S X N Z
P W S N V U L M D B V M Q U O W P T B Z P H V X
K M A E J J I L T A D V T N L G C R H I R W Q A
Q K U P T S P N N O I W T D L W Q U R L G T C L
D Z D R S C V E E G N A H C E T A M I L C V I P
R A Z I T D O H D Y K Y Y H G S U P R A I C N D
E G O V J O F N U O I S U E E Q B A T K Z S J Q
E N V A K P S A T M E D I C A R E F O R A L L B
S M D C O N H L S P S I D K Q D V T R U Y G W L
R K L Y S Z F B A A V P M S H N K R C H U U E C

SETH MOULTON
*UNITED STATES
REPRESENTATIVE FROM
MASSACHUSETTS*

STEVE BULLOCK
GOVERNOR OF MONTANA

MICHAEL BENNET

AGE IS JUST A NUMBER

A person must be at least 35 years old to serve as president. Luckily there's no upper limit! Match each Democratic candidate to the year in which they were born.

1) Pete Buttigieg   A) 1981

2) Elizabeth Warren   B) 1969

3) Tulsi Gabbard   C) 1982

4) Bernie Sanders   D) 1952

5) Cory Booker   E) 1949

6) Joe Biden   F) 1941

7) Marianne
   Williamson   G) 1942

Answer: 1) C, 2) E, 3) A, 4) F, 5) B, 6) G, 7) D

BERNIE SANDERS

WAYNE MESSAM

MAYOR OF MIRAMAR, FLORIDA

AMY KLOBUCHAR

POLITICAL MACHINE

Draw a new Democratic presidential candidate by melding these two candidates together. Will yours be white and male enough to alleviate electability concerns?

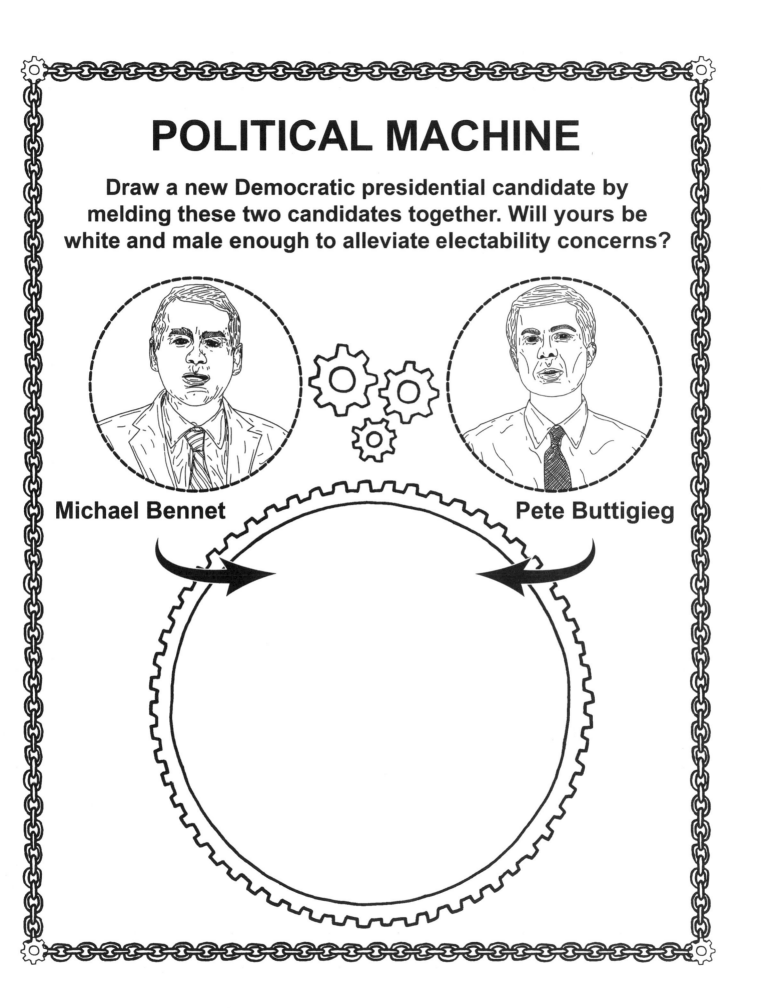

Michael Bennet

Pete Buttigieg

BETO O'ROURKE

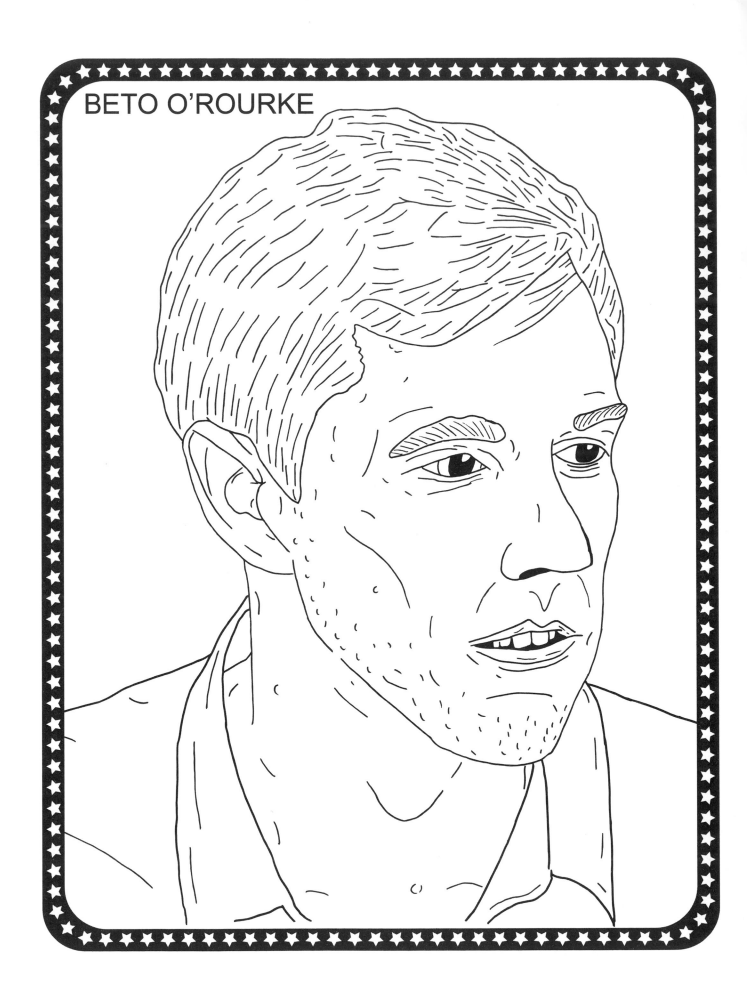

TULSI GABBARD
UNITED STATES REPRESENTATIVE
FROM HAWAII

JAY INSLEE
GOVERNOR OF WASHINGTON

TIM RYAN
UNITED STATES REPRESENTATIVE FROM OHIO

FRIENDS IN HIGH PLACES

**Celebrities love endorsing presidential candidates!
Using the famous names in the box, write each celebrity
below the candidate they've publicly endorsed.**

Tom Hanks	Cardi B
Lance Bass	Scarlett Johansson
George R. R. Martin	Dave Navarro
Rosie O'Donnell	Tommy Chong
Miley Cyrus	Tony! Toni! Toné!
Ron Perlman	Flea
Deepak Chopra	Mindy Kaling
Bill Nye	Rob Reiner

Pete Buttigieg   Elizabeth Warren   Bernie Sanders

_____   _____   _____

Joe Biden   Marianne Williamson   Andrew Yang

_____   _____   _____

Jay Inslee   Kamala Harris

_____   _____

Answer: Listen, I could tell you the correct answers, but what's the point? I mean really,
you should be voting for the person you think is most qualified to do the most good for our country.
Nonsense like celebrity endorsements are just a distraction from legitimate political debate.
Anyway, thanks for buying my book!

TOM STEYER

BILLIONAIRE,
HEDGE FUND MANAGER,
AND PHILANTHROPIST

ANDREW YANG

RICHARD OJEDA
FORMER STATE SENATOR
FROM WEST VIRGINIA

ELIZABETH WARREN

KAMALA HARRIS

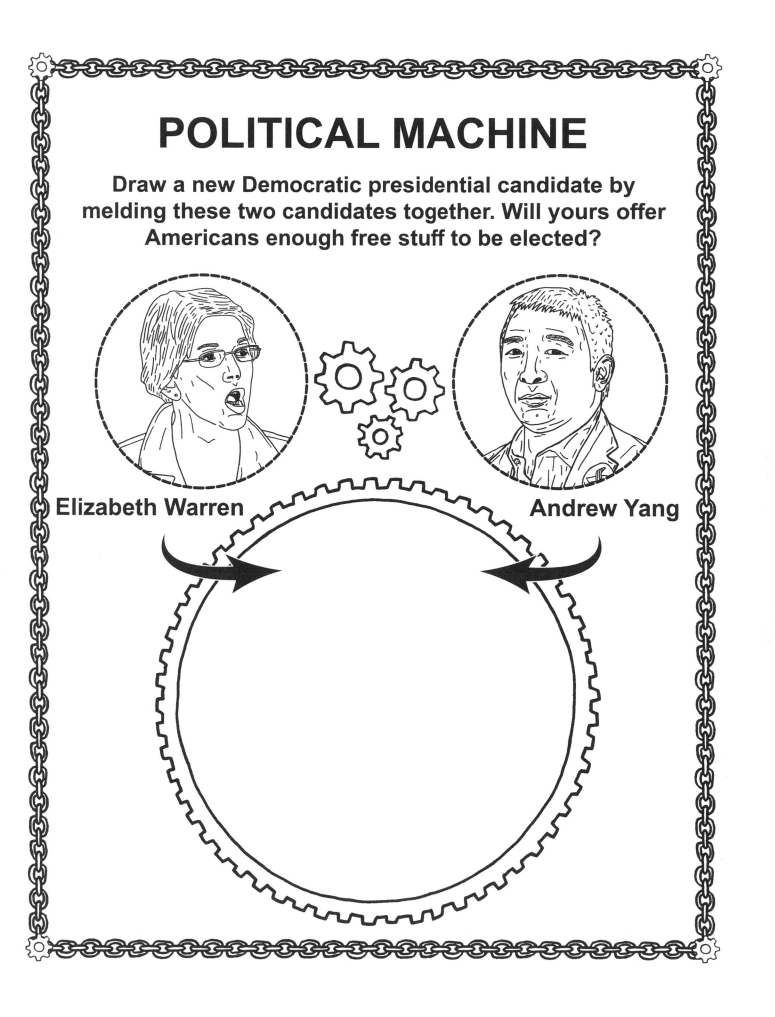

TULSI GABBARD

MIKE GRAVEL
FORMER UNITED STATES
SENATOR FROM ALASKA

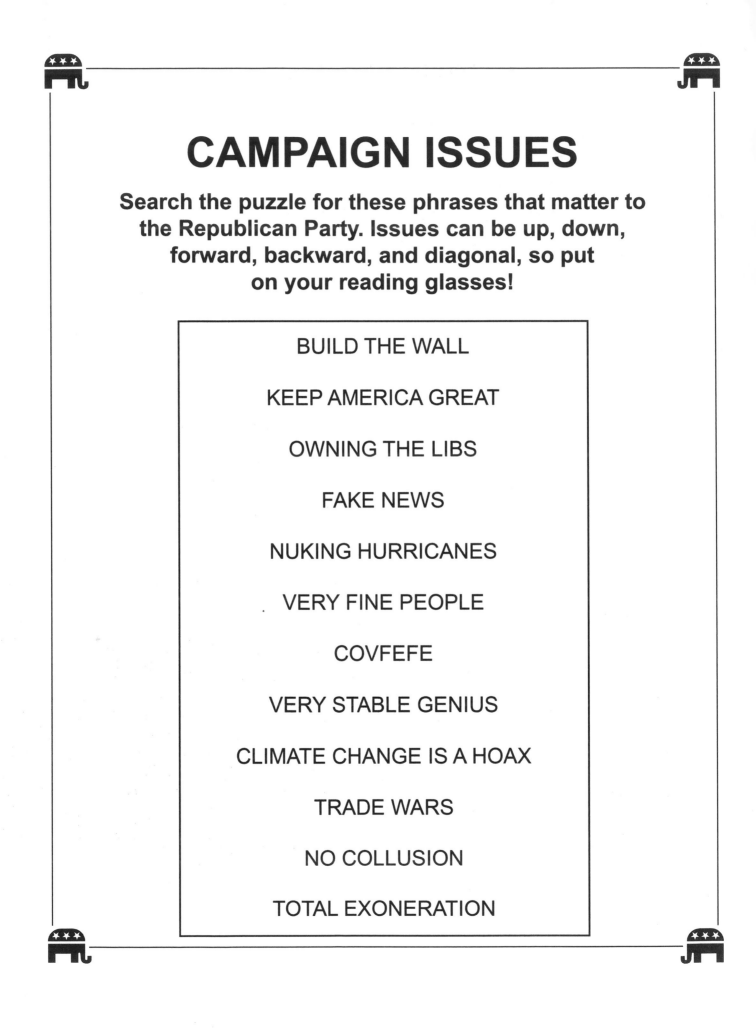

CAMPAIGN ISSUES

Search the puzzle for these phrases that matter to the Republican Party. Issues can be up, down, forward, backward, and diagonal, so put on your reading glasses!

BUILD THE WALL

KEEP AMERICA GREAT

OWNING THE LIBS

FAKE NEWS

NUKING HURRICANES

VERY FINE PEOPLE

COVFEFE

VERY STABLE GENIUS

CLIMATE CHANGE IS A HOAX

TRADE WARS

NO COLLUSION

TOTAL EXONERATION

```
I T I V W N O C O L L U S I O N O Z F C D T C T
W O Q N B U I L D T H E W A L L B I T M E O A I
Z S H V H W P I W S D N G J D X O V B G T T Y S
E N I Z A G A M P M U R T H T I W E M K N A P S
X I L F T E N A M A B O N P R S L R N Z E L U H
T O H S I R E T H G U A D Y M Y I Y G P D E P E
S J G S B I L E H T G N I N W O N F C H I X W A
G I A M T H E C H O S E N O N E G I M W S O X T
A B V F P F X H M D U I Y H A G N Z G E N W E
A Z O J E L E A U B A D H O M B R E S I R E S N
C C T F A K E N E W S Y H D S V E P I B P R I G
O E V T A E R G A C I R E M A P E E K U N A P O
J O W S R A W E D A R T S O L K N O Z I U T W K
C P Z Q Z E L I W R V D Z H I A M P K W C I J N
N R H E L H M S S C L E A N C O A L Y W W O M U
U V E R Y S T A B L E G E N I U S E R H W N L O
O N U K I N G H U R R I C A N E S V N Y D I T Y
Z J F F N T W O C O R I N T H I A N S S G D A W
E G A C C K L A T M O O R R E K C O L A L T R V
P W S Z S Y J X K K D E F T L W R P E I U H D Q
H R Q P C H O C O L A T E C A K E O T Z C Q Y D
J R L B U L M E W C F N S D M S N V E J L P Q V
P U K Y M S Z F O Y I J Y U C Q R A J C W A R K
M Y E L X F C X G I K B P Y W D O A B K C J C D
```

WAYNE MESSAM

BERNIE SANDERS

JOE BIDEN

MARIANNE
WILLIAMSON

PETE BUTTIGIEG

JAY INSLEE

POLITICAL MACHINE

Draw a new Democratic presidential candidate by melding these two candidates together. Will any American voters be able to recognize your candidate on the street?

Amy Klobuchar

Julián Castro

KAMALA HARRIS

STEVE BULLOCK

TIM RYAN

ANDREW YANG

BILL DE BLASIO

Can you unscramble these words?

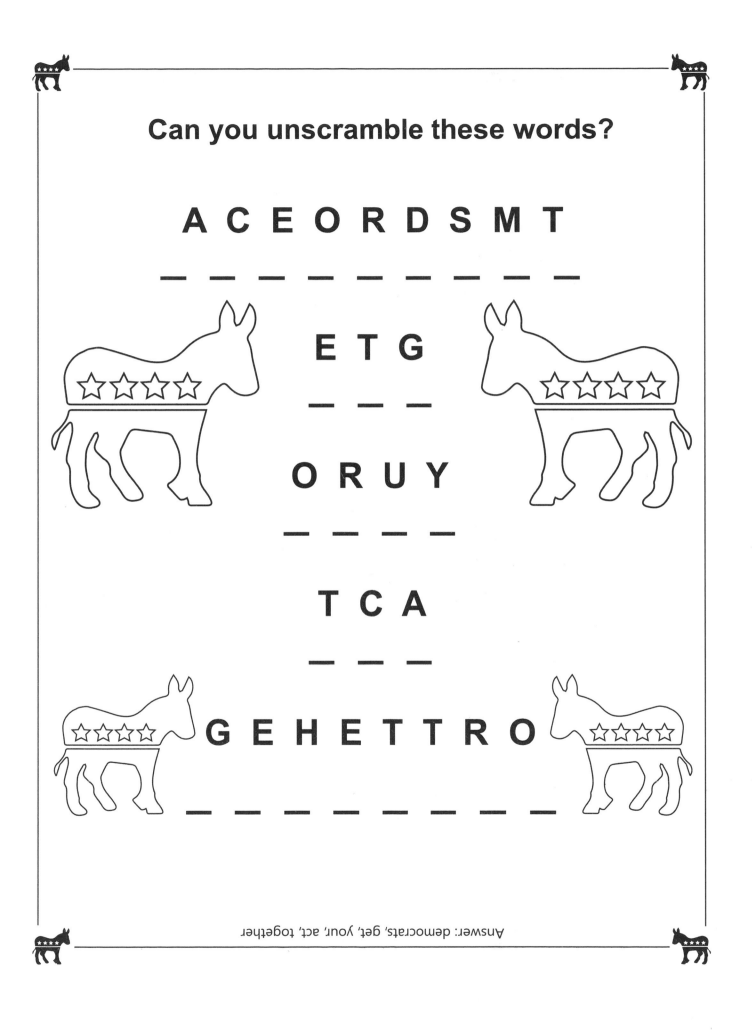

A C E O R D S M T

_ _ _ _ _ _ _ _ _ _

E T G

_ _ _

O R U Y

_ _ _ _

T C A

_ _ _

G E H E T T R O

_ _ _ _ _ _ _ _

ABOUT THE ARTIST

Sonya Saturday was born in Virginia and raised in Florida (both of which are in the USA) by a Democrat mother and a Republican father. She has drawn a bunch of books, including *The 2016 Republican Presidential Candidates Coloring and Activity Book*, which was kind of like this one but about Republicans instead! Sonya currently lives in Los Angeles, California, where she makes art and comics. Her website is sonyasaturday.com.